Introduction to Japan

Despite the export of its products to the rest of the world and a high international profile, Japan remains a mystery to many outsiders.

These densely populated islands have a unique culture in the world. Also, the Japanese are a homogeneous race with virtually no outside ethnic influences.

Japan's culture is based on centuries of tradition, while on the surface it looks like any modern society. Following the rules and avoiding individualism are very important.

For a very long time blind obedience to superiors was the overriding requirement of life in Japan. Central to this was reverence for the emperor. Today it is less so, but the royal family continues to be held in awe by the average Japanese.

Evidence of change is seen in the behaviour and attitudes of younger people. Although mild by Western norms, they are beginning to rebel against the standards of their parents.

People can visit Japan easily, but the nation does little to encourage tourism. The rest of the world is hugely important as a market place; however, Japan remains fiercely independent, taking in only those outside influences that suit it.

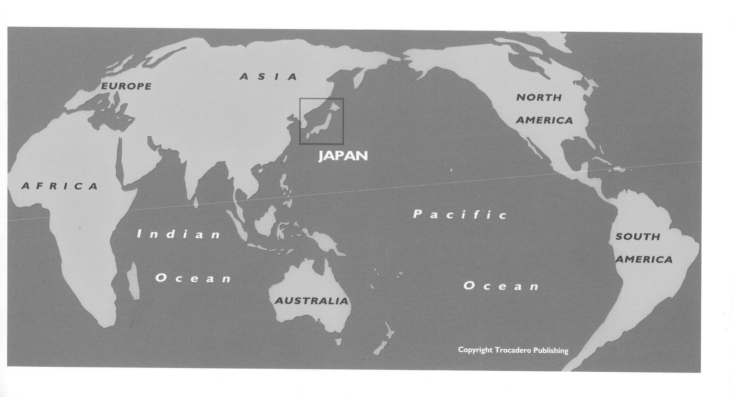

Government structure

Country name
Japan

Government type
Constitutional hereditary monarchy
with a parliamentary government

Capital
Tokyo

Head of state
Emperor (hereditary)

Head of government
Prime Minister
Holds office through support of a
majority of members of the Diet

Legislative branch
Diet
Bicameral parliament comprising
Shugi-in
(House of Representatives)
lower house, 480 members
elected for four-year term
Sangi-in
(House of Councillors)
upper house, 252 members
elected for six-year term

Administrative divisions
47 prefectures

National holiday
23 December
(Emperor Akihito's Birthday)

Constitution
Promulgated 3 May 1947

Legal system
Based on European civil law systems,
some English–American influences

Voting
20 years of age,
universal, non-compulsory

Until 1945 Japan lagged behind the rest of the world when it came to democracy. Through to the nineteenth century it had been mostly ruled by all-powerful shogun. At the same time the emperor was considered to be divine and commanded enormous respect from his subjects. The shogun men held the reins of power while permitting the emperor to rule as a figurehead.

The Meiji Restoration swept away the shogunate in 1867, bringing back the concept of a divine emperor ruling the nation. This was gradually tempered by the introduction of a parliament, known as the Diet and modelled on that of Prussia. As the emperor appointed all members of the upper house, he still wielded great power. Only the lower house was elected by the people.

The emperor retained his divine status until Japan's defeat in World War II. The Allied Occupation Force drafted a new constitution for Japan, permitting the emperor to remain as head of state, but as a constitutional monarch. The Diet became fully elected.

Viewed from outside, Japanese politics often seem chaotic. Part of the reason is the existence of more than 10 000 political parties, most with only small regional power bases. The conservative Liberal Democratic Party (LDP) has held government since 1955, except for a short break from 1993 to 1996. Its main opposition is the Social Democratic Party (SDP), although it

THE EMPEROR

To outsiders, the status of Japan's emperor has always been something of a mystery. Until 1945 all emperors were considered divine, that they were descended from the gods. This divinity officially ended in 1945; however, it does not prevent many Japanese still regarding the emperor with unquestioning respect and reverence.

Until recent years few Japanese had even seen the emperor. Almost none had ever heard him speak. When Emperor Hirohito broadcast to the nation following the surrender in 1945, there was profound shock right through the population.

Imperial reverence before 1945 took many forms. One example is the tram cars that passed the Imperial Palace in the centre of Tokyo. At a designated point they would halt so that all passengers could bow to the emperor, unseen behind high walls and thick foliage.

NEWSPIX — TOSHIFUMI KITAMURA

Akihito, the present Emperor of Japan

was in coalition with the LDP during the 1990s.

Each of Japan's forty-seven prefectures has its own regional government. There is an elected governor, and a unicameral assembly with all members elected by the people. A third level of elected government operates to administer towns and cities.

WWW.SOURCES
www.kantei.go.jp/foreign/server-e.html
Details of government structure, links to departments

www.mofa.go.jp
Ministry of Foreign Affairs site

www.asiadragons.com/japan/government_and_politics
Links to most government offices and organisations

Transport

SCOTT BRODIE

A Tokyo commuter train passes through the Shinjuku district

Public transport

Japan has a superbly developed network of public transport in its cities and towns. Most are efficiently run, clean and modern. They are capable of shifting vast numbers of commuters relatively quickly. Japanese people are heavy users of public transport.

Underground railways, known as subways, operate in many cities using electric trains that run either on steel tracks or with rubber wheels on concrete paths. All operate at short intervals throughout the day and into late evening. Subway carriages have electronic maps displaying the route and the train's progress between stations. Some lines are owned by the government, others are owned by private companies.

Supplementing the subways are comprehensive bus networks in all cities and smaller towns. Like the subways, buses carry an incredible number of people, cramming passengers in like sardines, especially at peak hours. A few cities, such as Hiroshima, continue to operate electric tram services. Tokyo has monorail and light-rail lines.

Japanese taxis are expensive, but well worth the money. Most drivers wear suit and tie, and the taxis are very clean and modern. The driver has a mechanism to open the door for passengers. Almost all taxis are Toyota Crowns or Nissan Cedrics that are specially designed for taxi work.

Rail

Japan's rail system is a shining example of the nation's dedication to efficiency. Virtually all parts of the country are linked by long-distance rail services, most of which are electrified.

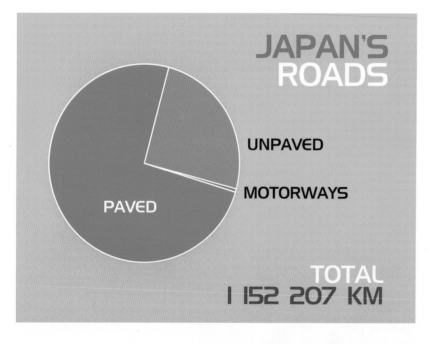

JAPAN'S ROADS

UNPAVED

MOTORWAYS

PAVED

TOTAL
1 152 207 KM

All operate on strict timetables that are maintained to the minute.

High-speed trains provide efficient links between airports and city centres as well. Shinkansen (bullet trains) ply the main trunk routes between Japanese cities at speeds up to 230 kilometres per hour. Shinkansen carriages are air-conditioned, with comfortable airline-type seats. They operate at very regular intervals, as close as fifteen minutes apart. New Shinkansen, called Nozomi, are being introduced. Nozomi travel in excess of 300 kilometres per hour — only the French TGV is faster.

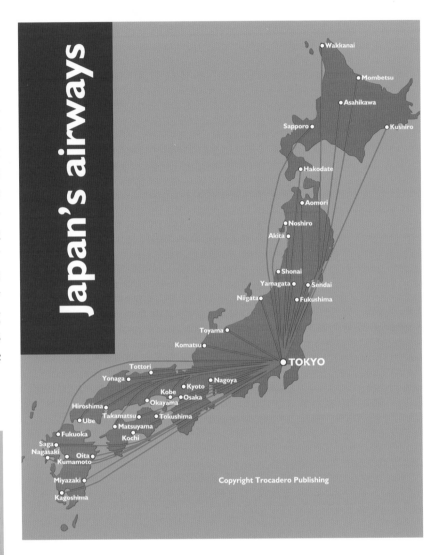

Japan's airways

Wakkanai
Mombetsu
Asahikawa
Sapporo
Kushiro
Hakodate
Aomori
Noshiro
Akita
Shonai
Yamagata
Sendai
Niigata
Fukushima
Toyama
Komatsu
Tottori
TOKYO
Yonaga
Nagoya
Kobe
Kyoto
Osaka
Okayama
Hiroshima
Takamatsu
Tokushima
Ube
Matsuyama
Fukuoka
Kochi
Saga
Nagasaki
Oita
Kumamoto
Miyazaki
Kagoshima

Copyright Trocadero Publishing

Freeways in Japan are crammed into every available space in the major cities

The Japanese rail system does not use trackside signals as in most other parts of the world. Instead, a computer in Tokyo transmits data to trains through the rails. Rail travel in Japan is very safe. As with the subways, the various rail services are a combination of government-owned (Japan Railways) and private-enterprise.

JAPAN'S MAIN PORTS AND HARBOURS

Akita
Amagasaki
Chiba
Hachinohe
Hakodate
Higashi-Harima
Himeji
Hiroshima
Kawasaki
Kinuura
Kobe
Kushiro
Mizushima
Moji
Nagoya
Osaka
Sakai
Sakaide
Shimizu
Tokyo
Tomakomai

Road

With such a huge number of people crammed into such a small area, travel by road in Japan can be very frustrating. Although vast networks of freeways have been constructed to aid traffic movement, in peak hours it is very slow. On the streets of the cities traffic flow is erratic, although the Japanese tend to drive in an orderly fashion most of the time.

As Japan is a major car-building nation, most Japanese families own, or aspire to own, a car. However, use of the family car can often be a curse, especially when such highly efficient public transport is available.

Aviation

Being such a small land mass, it could be expected that domestic air services would be limited in Japan. This is not so. Despite competition from Shinkansen, Japan's domestic airlines operate high-frequency shuttle services between all the major cities. Japan Airlines (JAL) and All Nippon Airways (ANA) fly specially modified Boeing 747 aircraft in all-economy class configurations, carrying more than 500 passengers each.

International air services are also operated by JAL and ANA. Airlines from all parts of the world operate frequent services to cities such as Tokyo, Osaka, Kyoto and Nagoya. A most interesting sight for travellers is the ground crew lining up and bowing to a departing aircraft as it is pushed back from the gate.

Tokyo's international airport at Narita is about a ninety-minute drive from the city centre. For decades legal challenges and protests have prevented

A driverless light-rail train carries passengers around new business precincts built on Tokyo's former dockland areas

A specially built car-carrier ship loads hundreds of vehicles for shipment to export markets

its expansion. Thus, while it is quite efficient, it is very congested. Osaka solved the problem of where to build by locating its Kansei Airport on an island of reclaimed land off the coast.

JAPAN'S SHIPPING FLEET
Bulk 137
Cargo 51
Chemical tanker 15
Combination bulk 22
Combination ore/oil 3
Container 22
Liquefied gas 49
Passenger 9
Passenger/cargo 2
Petroleum tanker 194
Refrigerated cargo 15
Roll-on roll-off 49
Short-sea passenger 6
Vehicle carrier 56

Shipping

Japan has been a maritime nation for centuries. It was trading with China, Korea and other South-east Asian lands well before the arrival of the first European traders in the sixteenth century. In the late nineteenth century, following the opening up of Japan to the rest of the world, Japan quickly adopted Western, especially British, maritime procedures.

Steamships ordered from Scottish shipyards were used on the world's shipping routes. At the same time, Japanese industrialists copied the techniques used to build these ships, creating Japan's own shipbuilding industry. Both civilian and naval ships were constructed, providing the nation with the power to take on and defeat the Russian fleet in 1905 and deliver a crippling blow to the US Navy in 1941.

After World War II, Japanese yards concentrated on building giant oil tankers and specialised carriers for ores and grains. Another Japanese speciality is the huge slab-sided cargo ships that carry cars and trucks to the markets of the world.

www.sources
www.jal.co.jp/e
Japan Air Lines site

www.japan-guide.com/e/e2019.html
History of railways in Japan

www.geocities.com/TheTropics/Cove/5750
Information about Japanese railways

www.traveladdicts.connectfree.co.uk/Japan/Transport.htm
Experiences using Japanese public transport

Communications

JAPAN'S TELEPHONE USAGE

TOTAL POPULATION

TELEPHONE LINES INSTALLED

CELLULAR TELEPHONES IN USE

0 MILLIONS 30   60   90   120   150

Telecommunications

With such a sophisticated electronics industry, it is only to be expected that telecommunications in Japan are of a very high standard. Since the 1970s Japan has led the way in many developments in communications. However, it has been outstripped in mobile cellular telephone manufacturing by European companies.

Most Japanese homes have at least one telephone line, and the use of mobile telephones is very widespread. International telecommunications use both undersea cables and satellite. There are cable links to China, Russia, the Philippines and North America and on to the rest of the world. Earth stations provide services through the Inmarsat, Intelsat and Intersputnik satellites.

Radio and Television

Ownership of radio receivers is extensive, with almost one for every person. The AM system is the predominant mode for broadcasters, with close to 200 stations around the country. FM is not as popular as in other countries, with only twenty-four stations nationally.

Television viewing is an integral part of Japanese life. There is one television receiver for every two people. A wide variety of networks generates thousands of hours of programming every day, almost all in the Japanese language. The exceptions are cable or satellite broadcasts from other countries. The United States military operates a television network for service personnel stationed in Japan.

Internet

The internet is freely available to all Japanese who wish to use it. Around twenty-seven million people access it on a regular basis. Much of this is from home, school or office computers; however, internet cafés are to be found everywhere in the cities and towns.

www.sources

www.yusei.go.jp/eng
Details of telecommunications in Japan

www.japan-guide.com/e/e2075.html
About TV in Japan, links to broadcasters

www.virtualokinawa.com/afn/
American forces network, Okinawa

Industry: primary and secondary

Japan's primary industry accounts for less than two per cent of the gross national product. However, the government offers large subsidies to agricultural producers and places high tariff barriers on some

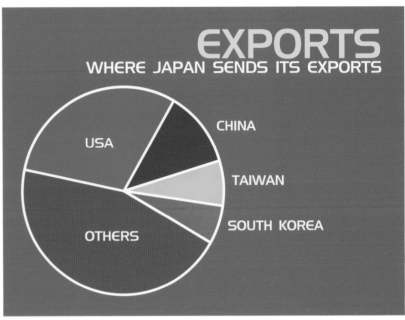

EXPORTS
WHERE JAPAN SENDS ITS EXPORTS

USA

CHINA

TAIWAN

SOUTH KOREA

OTHERS

agricultural imports, particularly rice. Japanese fishing fleets ply the oceans of the world to satisfy the huge home market for seafood.

Like most Asian nations, Japan's initial development of secondary industry in the late nineteenth century centred on textiles. Before long, however, manufacturing had expanded into shipbuilding and other heavy industries. It was common practice for

Japan has a huge fishing industry, with large boats that range across the Pacific and Indian Oceans

JAPAN'S EXPORTS
US$450 billion

Main exports
office equipment, chemicals, semi-conductors, motor vehicles

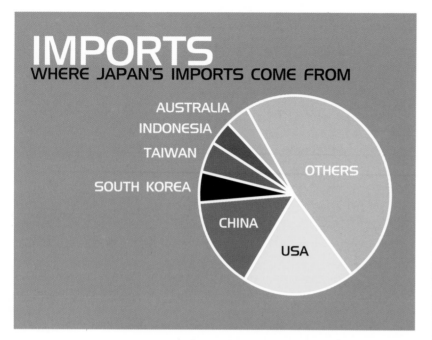

IMPORTS
WHERE JAPAN'S IMPORTS COME FROM

AUSTRALIA
INDONESIA
TAIWAN
SOUTH KOREA
OTHERS
CHINA
USA

Japanese manufacturers to identify the best products in the world, then copy them and ultimately make a better version.

Following World War II, industries that had fed the Japanese war machine turned to producing civilian

Until recently, Japanese were enthusiastic consumers of an ever-widening range of products from the nation's manufacturers

products. A vast range of small manufactures, from toys to stereo systems, poured out of Japanese factories and into homes around the world in the 1960s. Cars and electrical goods led the way. Brands such as Nissan, Mazda,

Much of Japan's car-building industry today uses robots on the production lines

Despite being chronically inefficient, rice farming continues in Japan under heavy government protection

JAPAN'S MAIN SECONDARY INDUSTRIES
**motor vehicles
electronic equipment
machine tools
steel and non-ferrous metals
ships
chemicals
textiles
processed foods**

on high-technology products. Commonly, the research, development and design work are done in Japan, but the goods are manufactured in Japanese-owned factories in Thailand, Malaysia and Indonesia, where labour costs are lower.

Toyota, Panasonic, Sony and Akai became well known.

Much of Japan's heavy industry is concentrated in southern Honshu island and northern Kyushu. The major industrial centres are Yokohama, Tokyo, Kobe, Nagoya and Osaka.

As labour costs rose, manufacture of cheap products all but ceased. Japan's corporations today concentrate

JAPAN'S IMPORTS
US$355 billion

**Main imports
textiles, chemicals, fuels,
foodstuffs, minerals**

www.sources
web.mit.edu/mit-japan/Products/videos/93-01.html
Overview of Japanese manufacturing

www.jsc.org.uk/history/hstry07.htm
History of Japanese shipbuilding

mcel.pacificu.edu/as/students/jcars/home.html
Japanese motor industry history

www.corporateinformation.com/jpsector/Electronics.html
Japanese electronics industry

JAPAN'S PRIMARY INDUSTRIES
sugar beets, vegetables, dairy products, poultry, pork, eggs, fish, rice, fruit

Geography, environment and climate

Japan comprises four main islands — Honshu, Hokkaido, Shikoku and Kyushu — plus many smaller islands, including Okinawa to the south. The landscape is very beautiful, with deep valleys and soaring mountains, and numerous waterways and lakes. Many of the mountains are volcanic. All the main islands are densely populated. The Tokyo–Yokohama region is the most populous on Earth. Japan's mineral resources are poor: materials for manufacturing, such as iron ore and coal, are imported.

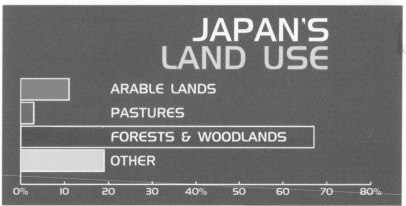

The majesty of the sacred Mount Fuji

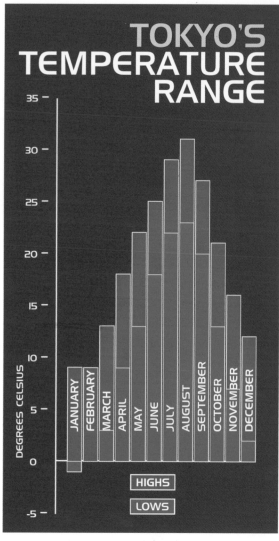

TOKYO'S TEMPERATURE RANGE

DEGREES CELSIUS

- 35
- 30
- 25
- 20
- 15
- 10
- 5
- 0
- -5

JANUARY, FEBRUARY, MARCH, APRIL, MAY, JUNE, JULY, AUGUST, SEPTEMBER, OCTOBER, NOVEMBER, DECEMBER

HIGHS

LOWS

Japanese winters are very cold, winds from the Asian mainland blowing snow across most of the islands. By contrast, Pacific winds make summers warm and often very humid. Rainfall is usually heavy through most of

JAPAN'S LAND USE

- ARABLE LANDS
- PASTURES
- FORESTS & WOODLANDS
- OTHER

0% 10 20 30 40% 50 60 70 80%

JAPAN'S SIZE

Total area
374 744 sq. km
Coastline 29 751 km
Border countries
none

JAPAN'S LOCATION
Latitude   36°N
Longitude 138°E

the year. Typhoons often sweep in from the surrounding oceans, bringing parts of the country to a halt for days. One frightening aspect of life in Japan is the frequency of earthquakes. These vary from minor tremors, lasting less than a minute, to devastating movements that destroy entire cities.

Rapid industrial growth after the 1950s created highly polluting factories. Discharges of toxic materials into waterways reached scandalous proportions in the late 1960s. Much of Japan's power generation is by oil-fired plants; combined with coal-powered factories,

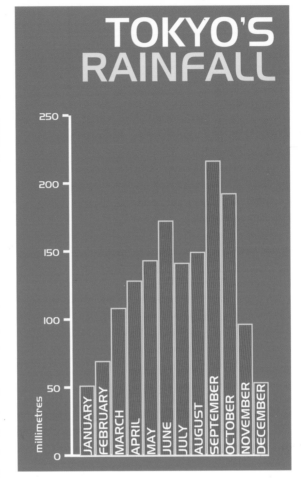

TOKYO'S RAINFALL

these have created significant levels of air pollution. Acid rain, which pollutes waterways and kills marine life, is a major problem. Also, Japanese consumers love highly packaged goods, creating a massive disposal problem.

The aftermath of the 1948 Fukui earthquake, in which 3500 people died

Peoples and daily life

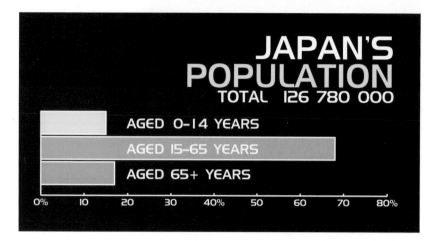

JAPAN'S POPULATION
TOTAL 126 780 000

AGED 0-14 YEARS

AGED 15-65 YEARS

AGED 65+ YEARS

0% 10 20 30 40% 50 60 70 80%

Japan is a very ethnically homogeneous society. The only significant non-Japanese groups are Koreans and a tiny number of Ainu people on the island of Hokkaido. The Ainu are gradually integrating with the Japanese and will probably be indistinguishable in a hundred years. Koreans and Ainu together amount to less than one per cent of the population.

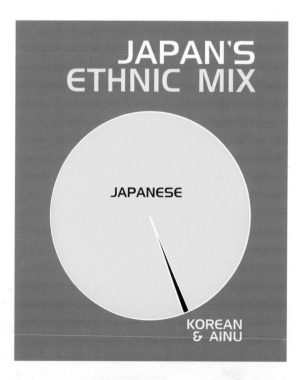

JAPAN'S ETHNIC MIX

JAPANESE

KOREAN & AINU

With 3300 people for each square kilometre of land, Japan has one of the highest residential densities in the world. By comparison, the figure for the United States is twenty-eight. Because of this crowding, the Japanese have had to develop social structures that provide individuals with a degree of privacy or personal space, even in public.

While some Japanese still live in traditional timber homes, most are now high-rise apartment-block dwellers. These large complexes with hundreds of homes are packed into the suburban areas of each Japanese city. The immense urban sprawl of the cities means travel to work can take up to two hours, even on high-speed commuter trains.

Before 1945 Japan's education structure was not comprehensive. The Allied Occupation Forces created a system of universal education in the late 1940s — education became compulsory, free and available to all Japanese children for the first time. Today education is an obsession. Most students remain in school well beyond the compulsory nine years. As well as daytime school, many students attend additional evening classes to improve their chances in examinations.

Life for adult Japanese revolves around work. Employment structures are rigid and hierarchical. Until the 1990s most Japanese expected to stay with the one company all their working lives. Loyalty to the employer was strong, even though workplace systems

Playing pachinko

were often bureaucratic and inefficient. As the economy slowed in the 1990s, large corporations began retrenching workers. Most Japanese did not know how to handle such a situation.

Japan's economic miracle was greatly aided by the thrifty habits of its people. Despite miserly interest rates, Japanese maintain healthy balances in their bank accounts. In the 1960s and 1970s this created a vast pool of finance that was loaned to expanding industries.

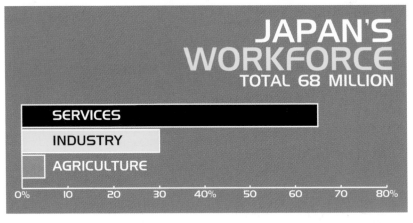

JAPAN'S WORKFORCE
TOTAL 68 MILLION

SERVICES							
INDUSTRY							
AGRICULTURE							
0%	10	20	30	40%	50	60	70	80%

Crowds throng Tokyo's Shibuya shopping district

Leisure time for most Japanese is limited. They are keen followers of baseball and sumo wrestling. Others spend hours playing a pinball game called pachinko in vast halls. Movies are popular, both local productions and those from the West. Large theme parks such as Tokyo Disneyland attract millions of visitors.

www.sources
cheno.com/job/career/workinjp.html
Working in Japan

papa.essortment.com/wrestlingsumoh_rvqp.htm
History of sumo wrestling

mcel.pacificu.edu/as/students/pachinko/index2.html
All about playing pachinko

Religion and beliefs

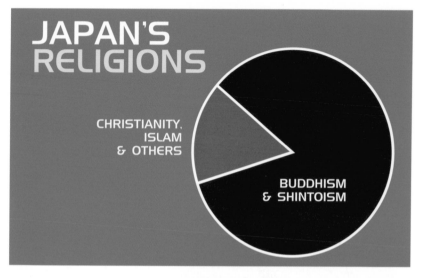

JAPAN'S RELIGIONS

CHRISTIANITY, ISLAM & OTHERS

BUDDHISM & SHINTOISM

Statue of Buddha at Kamakura

Most Japanese are adherents to both Shintoism and Buddhism simultaneously. A small number are practising Christians. Shinto, the indigenous religion of Japan, evolved in ancient times. Its dominance was substantially reduced in the sixth century by the introduction of Buddhism from China. Buddhism proved so popular that Shinto was forced to adapt in order to survive.

Unlike most other religions, Shinto evolved rather than being founded by one or more people. It came from the beliefs and fears of a simple people thousands of years ago. Most traditions and aspects of Japanese culture have some relationship with Shinto. There are no sacred texts. The objects of worship are natural elements such as mountains, the sun and trees. The famous Mount Fuji is considered sacred by Shinto. As well, ancestors and national figures may become objects of worship.

www.sources

www.japan-guide.com/e/e629.html
Details of Japan's religions

acro.harvard.edu/GEI/japan.html
Japanese shrines and temples

www.japan-zone.com/omnibus/other_religion.shtml
Christianity in Japan

Food and cuisine

Food in Japan ranges from horrendously expensive restaurant meals to the simplest snacks in railway station kiosks. While ingredients are important, as with most aspects of life in Japan much emphasis is placed on presentation.

Rice is the staple food for everyone, and accompanies most meals. The most popular meals are sashimi, sushi and tempura. Japanese cuisine evolved to suit the available ingredients. This is why there is a great deal of emphasis on rice, vegetables and fish, rather than meat. Most meats are imported and usually very expensive.

Many cafés and restaurants specialise in a particular type of food. They can be very good at delivering meals quickly and efficiently to cater for workers in their lunch breaks. Restaurants commonly have window displays of the meals they sell, packaged in moulded plastic containers.

Many people, particularly the younger ones, have taken enthusiastically to Western-style fast foods. Fast-food chains such as McDonalds and KFC have a large presence in Japan, albeit with menus adapted to suit local tastes.

Another interesting aspect of Japanese life is vending machines. They are everywhere — in the streets, in arcades, on railway stations. They dispense all sorts of foods and drinks and are heavily patronised.

When the first tea was introduced to Japan by Buddhist monks, it was greatly revered because of its rarity. Special rituals grew up around its preparation and drinking. By the fifteenth century a formal tea ceremony had been developed to be carried out in a special tea house. Invited guests sat around a fire over which hung a pot. A tea master prepared the drink slowly, with elaborate ritual, before passing it to guests to consume reverently.

POPULAR JAPANESE DISHES

Sashimi
raw fish
Sushi
cold rice garnished with raw fish
Tempura
deep-fried seafood and vegetables
Yakitori
grilled chicken on skewers
Okonomiyaki
a cross between pizza and pancake
Gyoza
dumplings
Shabu Shabu
fondue meats
Nikujaga
meat with potato
Tonkatsu
deep-fried pork cutlet
Natto
fermented soybeans
Nabe
hotpot meals eaten communally
Oden
fish cakes, eggs and vegetables in a soup
Miso Soup
soup made with soybeans

www.sources
japanesefood.about.com
All about Japanese food

jin.jcic.or.jp/kidsweb/cook/intro/intro.html
Introduction to Japanese cooking

www.amphi.com/~psteffen/fmf/food.htm
Basic Japanese food and culture of eating

Arts, crafts and literature

rom the fifth century Japanese intellectuals enthusiastically embraced literature, dance, music and other arts imported from China. Traditional music evolved initially from Shinto ceremonies. Instruments were introduced to Japan from China, Korea and western Asia by traders. This led to the evolution of instruments such as flutes and stringed instruments that suited Japanese tastes.

Early Japanese literature was heavily influenced by Buddhist texts, most imported from China. Early writers even created their works in Chinese. At first, poetry was the strongest of the literary forms with varying styles evolving over the centuries. This gradually evolved into the writing of fiction some 1000 years ago.

As with music, Japanese drama originated in Shinto ceremonies. Styles

Part of the large cast of a
Kabuki performance

include gigaku, gyodo, sangaku, saru-gaku and bugaku. The most famous of all drama styles are no and kabuki. No originated in the fourteenth century, using song and dance to relate traditional Japanese stories. Kabuki's origins are very different. Initially based on religious themes, it soon moved into the erotic and was often performed by prostitutes. After its banning in the seventeenth century, kabuki returned in a much sanitised form concentrating on drama with dialogue.

From earliest times Japanese artists endeavoured to provide a spiritual sense in what they painted. It was

A character from a No play

Gardens play a key role in the Shinto religion. Great emphasis is placed on tranquillity, providing a place for meditation. With so little space available, landscaping became a special art of creating nature in miniature in urban spaces. Bonsai, the art of growing miniature trees, first began a thousand years ago. Enthusiasts constantly replant and trim the trees, to create a botanical sculpture. Fine specimens have been kept alive for hundreds of years.

Ikebana, the art of flower arranging, began as a religious ceremony. It soon developed into a popular pursuit, with millions engaged in arranging flowers for everyone's appreciation. There are many special Ikebana contests and festivals.

A classic piece of bonsai art

more about ideas and feelings than literal presentations of images. Another popular art form was silk-screening. Artists developed intricate designs from parchment, printing them on silk with hand-operated frames.

www.sources

www.fix.co.jp/kabuki/kabuki.html
Details of kabuki theatre and tradition

mockingbird.creighton.edu/english/worldlit/wldocs/japan.htm
Guide to Japanese literature

www.encyclopedia.com/printablenew/00807.html
History of Japanese drama

History and politics

LONELY PLANET IMAGES — OLIVER STREWE

Kinkaju-ji, the Golden Temple at Kyoto

The first arrivals

Accurate records of Japanese society began only 1600 years ago. However, well before then, the Ainu arrived in Japan from Korea or Manchuria. They were a simple people, engaged in fishing, hunting and some agriculture. Today only a small community remains, living on Hokkaido.

Around 1900 years ago another race, quite different from the Ainu, arrived on the Japanese islands from the Asian mainland, probably from Korea. More advanced, and skilled in working with bronze and iron, they soon overran the Ainu. They were the basis of today's Japanese society.

Growth of Yamato

By the fifth century a system of uji (clans) had developed. They were mainly geographically based. Uji were very hierarchical, with groups of related families taking the leadership roles and a king–priest at the top.

Gradually one uji, the Yamato, gained influence over others in the central and western regions. Yamato's base was initially at Nara. This expansion occurred mostly by force and laid the groundwork for Japan's ruling structure. The Yamato leader was acknowledged as emperor, controlling taxation, the military and other key aspects of society.

The divine emperor

Soon there emerged the concept of the emperor as a divine being. The Yamato emperor claimed descent from Amaterasu Omikami, the sun goddess. He expected his subjects not only to obey him, but also to worship him as a god. This unyielding structure remained in place until 1945.

Cultural development

Early Japanese society was modelled on that of China. Yamato endeavoured to put in place a centralised administration like China's. Intellectuals studied and emulated all things Chinese, adapting them to Japanese uses. Japanese architecture, dress, calligraphy and arts all have roots in Chinese culture.

Also from China came Buddhism, around 1400 years ago. At first there was a cultural clash between Buddhism and Shinto, Japan's indigenous religion. Although Buddhism was adopted by the Yamato court as its official religion, many uji clung to Shinto.

Rise of Fujiwara

Yamato ruled without opposition until the mid-ninth century, when the imperial court became dominated by the Fujiwara clan. Previously just one of many uji, the politically astute Fujiwara married into the ruling family. They left the emperor in place but manipulated his every action from behind the scenes, supported by Buddhist priests.

Although Fujiwara controlled the court of the emperor, they could not always impose their will on daimyo (uji leaders), particularly those far from the capital. Daimyo maintained a military force called samurai (those who serve) to protect farmers and others from harassment. In return the daimyo expected a share of the produce or other services. This was the basis of the long-lasting Japanese feudal system.

Civil war

Fujiwara's strategy of intermarriage in the ruling classes produced many descendants. The more distant of these, known as Taira or Minamoto, were banished from the capital. In the provinces they gained such power they would eventually challenge Fujiwara. Civil war raged for most of the twelfth century as the rivals jockeyed for power.

Taira gained power in the early 1100s under emperor Kiyomori. However, by 1185 Minamoto had defeated Taira in battle. Yorimoto, daimyo of Minamoto, set up a capital at Kamakura, near present-day Tokyo.

The Hojo

Yorimoto founded a military regime, taking the title of shogun (commander-in-chief for the suppression of barbarians) in 1192. He maintained the myth that the emperor was in control. On Yorimoto's death in 1199 his sons, unable to control the daimyo, were assassinated. The Hojo took control of the country.

The Hojo preferred to manipulate power from behind the scenes. Various Fujiwara were appointed as shogun, although under tight restraint. Hojo, whose control lasted until 1333, gave Japan a new legal system. Also during the Hojo reign two invasions by Kublai Khan's Mongol forces were successfully repelled.

A seppuku ceremony — the Samurai on the left prepares to commit ritual suicide

A Christian service in Japan

Ashikaga

Constantly diverted by the prospect of another Mongol invasion, the Hojo administration became shaky. The emperor, Go-Daigo, exploited his popularity with the people to stage two attempts, in 1324 and 1331, to reinstate imperial rule. Sent into exile, he was replaced by one of his more compliant relatives.

Go-Daigo returned from exile in 1333 when daimyo Ashikaga Takauiji deposed Hojo. The emperor abolished all shogunates and daimyo and tried to disperse their samurai, seeking a return to total imperial power. Takauiji's reaction was to remove Go-Daigo from power once again.

The Ashikaga took Kyoto as their capital, with Takauiji as shogun, but failed to consolidate their power. The daimyo began fighting among themselves. Life for ordinary Japanese became chaotic and bandits roamed the countryside.

Battles for control

By the early 1500s Japan had split into several autonomous regions, each under the control of a daimyo. Each daimyo was manoeuvring to become shogun. Oda Nobunaga of Owari province captured Kyoto in 1568, routing the Ashikaga and butchering thousands of Buddhist monks. His dictatorship lasted until 1582.

After Nobunaga came Toyotomi Hideyoshi, who spent much of his time reuniting the land. He corralled the samurai in castles close to the daimyo who controlled them. By 1590 his rule was close to absolute, with most daimyo united behind him, either voluntarily or not. On his death in 1598 he left a five-year-old boy as his successor.

Trading links

During this time Japan began developing international trade. Japanese ships plied Asian waters, creating links with China, Korea and South-east Asia. Japanese seafarers also became notorious as bloodthirsty pirates preying on traders in the region.

Tokugawa

With a five-year-old unable to run the country, the daimyo once more battled for control. This time, fortunately, it was Tokugawa Ieyasu who claimed victory in 1600. His base was Kanto province, with a capital at Edo (now Tokyo).

To secure their support, Tokugawa allowed the other daimyo free rein to run their provinces, providing they swore total allegiance to him. Those who did not found their wives and children held hostage at Edo to secure their compliance.

Toyotomi Hideyoshi

Tokugawa was adept at ensuring his officials never gained too much power or influence. He divided society into daimyo, samurai, peasants, artisans and merchants — a rigid class structure based on Confucian ideals.

Trade and Christianity

Portuguese traders first reached Japan in 1543. Before long they were trading Chinese silk to Japan. They also sold the Japanese a wide range of European goods, including guns, lacquerware and copper products, in return for silver. Portugal soon had well-established trading centres at Hirado and Nagasaki.

Traders were closely followed in 1549 by Catholic missionaries. Francis Xavier landed on Kyushu and was soon converting people to the faith. Despite opposition from Shinto and Buddhist priests, the missionary work expanded rapidly.

In the late sixteenth century the Spanish arrived, planning to break Portugal's monopoly. The church was working with the merchants, with disguised Franciscan missionaries arriving on the first ships.

The last of the Europeans to arrive were the British, in 1613. They were encouraged by a British sailor, Will Adams, who had been shipwrecked on the coast in 1600. He became a confidant of Tokugawa Ieyasu, teaching the shogun mathematics and Western-style shipbuilding.

Suppressing Christianity

Christianity's rise was concerning Japan's leadership as early as the 1580s. Toyotomi Hideyoshi ordered all Christian missionaries out of the country, but many disobeyed. In 1597 he retaliated by executing missionaries who had been openly converting Japanese in Kyoto and Osaka.

Tokugawa Ieyasu outlawed Christianity completely in 1614. Within four years severe persecution of Christians had become commonplace.

The closed kingdom

Shogun Tokugawa Iemitsu, in 1639, halted all foreign arrivals in Japan. He embarked on a campaign to return the nation to values that had prevailed before the Europeans sailed into view. Japanese were forbidden to travel overseas. Only a tiny handful of Dutch, Korean and Chinese were permitted to remain in Nagasaki to trade.

The Perry mission

For 200 years Japan remained all but closed to the outside world. On 8 July 1853 three United States Navy ships arrived in Tokyo Bay. One was a steamship, something the Japanese had never seen before. The leader of the mission, Commodore Matthew Perry, had orders to force Japan to open ports for trade with the United States.

Perry departed when the Japanese refused to allow him to land. On 13 February 1854 he returned with a well-armed fleet of eight ships. This time force of arms convinced the Japanese to relent. Following tortuous negotiations the Treaty of Kanagawa was signed on 31 March 1854, giving the United States what it wanted. Soon afterwards the same concessions were granted to European powers.

Internal dissent

There was shock and outrage that the shogun had conceded so much. Although a minority saw

the chance to modernise and industrialise, most favoured expulsion of all foreigners. Attacks on foreigners brought severe retaliation: warships bombarded ports, killing many locals.

An anti-shogun group of fanatical samurai was formed by the daimyo of Chushu, Hizen, Tosa and Satsuma provinces, as well as various nobles in the imperial court. Their plan was to depose the shogun and restore full imperial power. They were successful in 1867, when the new shogun, Tokugawa Yoshinobu, came to power. Faced with internal division and external pressures, he agreed to step down on 13 November.

Meiji Restoration

Thus began the Meiji Restoration. The under-age Emperor Mutsuhito ruled with the help of a range of advisers. Japan once more was under the control of an absolute monarch, a person considered by his subjects to be divine. The imperial capital moved from Kyoto to Edo, which was renamed Tokyo.

Within four years the feudal system was dismantled. Each daimyo handed over his lands to the emperor, enabling widespread land reform.

The samurai, disarmed and pensioned off, took it badly. They staged minor revolts against the emperor, all of which failed dismally. To neutralise them, compulsory military service was introduced. The Imperial Japanese Army was equipped with Western-style uniforms and armaments.

Foreign expertise was recruited to develop a modern infrastructure. Telegraphic communication was

Admiral Perry's mission in 1854

introduced and a railway line opened in 1872, linking Tokyo with Yokohama. While early railways were built with British assistance, the Japanese soon learned to do it for themselves. Ships bought from Scottish shipyards were copied to establish Japan's own shipbuilding industry.

Democracy

Initially ignoring calls for democracy, the emperor then tried to suppress them. When neither tactic worked, in 1880 Ito Hirobumi was directed to produce a new constitution that preserved the powers of the emperor.

In 1890 a parliament, called the Diet, was established with two houses. The lower house was elected by the people, the upper house appointed by the emperor.

Colonialism

The restoration of imperial power brought a surge in nationalism. Japan joined the European powers in their quest for colonial domination. War was declared against China in 1894, resulting in the taking of the Pescadore Islands, Formosa (Taiwan) and the Liao Tung region in Manchuria.

In the early twentieth century Czarist Russia was expanding ever eastward. Supported by a pact with Britain, Japan demanded that Russia relinquish its claims to Korea. Russia refused, so Japan declared war in 1904. The world was stunned when the Japanese forces defeated the Russian navy.

Korea and Shandong

In 1910 Japan officially annexed Korea, primarily to secure control of its vast mineral deposits. They would feed Japan's ever-growing industrial complex.

During the Great War (1914–18) Japan joined the Allies against Germany and the Austro–Hungarian empire. It occupied German territory on the Shandong peninsula in China. Next, Japan successfully demanded China give it major economic concessions in Manchuria and Inner Mongolia.

The foreign quarter at Yokohama in the late nineteenth century

Nationalism

In the 1920s the emphasis on colonial expansion was reduced and military power was curbed. Increasingly, political influence lay with the zaibatsu (business organisations). Economic growth was temporarily halted by the devastating earthquake of 1923, which destroyed most of the Tokyo–Yokohama region.

The downgrading of military power led many officers to form or join secret societies. Their plan was to establish a military dictatorship. The steady growth of unionism and communism was also concerning them.

Military revolt

Elements of the military in Manchuria sought a return to expansionism. Without official support from Tokyo they attacked Chinese troops near Shenyang (then known as Mukden). They had captured most of Manchuria by 1933.

Many supported the rebel army, believing the Western powers were trying to destroy their country. Prime Minister Inukai Tsuyoshi, who wanted

to stop the army's actions, was assassinated in May 1932. Subsequent years saw a series of weak governments. A coup d'état staged in February 1936 was eventually put down after several ministers were assassinated.

On 7 July 1937, following a clash with Chinese troops near Beijing, the Japanese swept through northern China capturing Nanjing, Beijing and Shanghai. Troops committed many atrocities against civilians, including bayoneting, beheading, rape and looting.

The Co-Prosperity Sphere

Finally, in 1940, the military took control of Japan. An admirer of Hitler, Minister for the Army General Tojo Hideki proposed a partnership with Germany and Italy. Subsequently he floated the idea of Japan taking control of France's Indo-Chinese colonies and the Dutch East Indies.

Tojo developed the idea of the Greater East Asia Co-Prosperity Sphere. Japan would rule and Japanese business would exploit the mineral and other wealth of the lands. In September 1940 Japan occupied Indo-China. The following month Tojo became prime minister.

The United States imposed an embargo on the sale of oil, iron, rubber and steel to Japan. This only encouraged the militarists. It was now urgent that Japan take control of Malaya for its rubber and Borneo for its oil, they argued fervently.

An audience with the Meiji emperor, who is partly concealed behind a screen

Allied commanders surrender to the Japanese at Singapore in February 1942

Launching the Sphere

Admiral Isoruko Yamamoto convinced Tojo it was essential that the US Navy fleet in Hawaii be destroyed. By the time it could be re-established, the Co-Prosperity Sphere would be reality. On Sunday 7 December 1941 six aircraft carriers dispatched their aircraft to attack military installations in Hawaii. Much of the Seventh Fleet was destroyed at its moorings; however, three aircraft carriers were at sea at the time.

Simultaneously, forces attacked Wake Island, Hong Kong, the Philippines and Malaya. By the middle of 1942 territory as far south as New Guinea had been captured. The triumphant advance was halted in the Papua New Guinean jungles and the Coral Sea, as the Allied fightback commenced.

The Japanese occupation of eastern Asia was marked by brutality and widespread atrocities. Local peoples and prisoners-of-war were treated barbarically. They were starved and beaten by Japanese guards in hellish prison camps. Many were made to work as slave labourers.

The slow retreat

Gradually, between 1942 and 1945, Allied forces pushed the dogged Japanese back. Vast numbers of Japanese and American soldiers and marines died in horrific battles for tiny Pacific atolls. In Manila thousands died in house-to-house fighting. At sea the battle was mostly fought with aircraft carriers and submarines.

In 1945 the taking of Okinawa enabled the Allies to unleash a sustained bombing campaign against Japanese cities. For the first time the horror of war was brought home to the Japanese population.

Realising an invasion of Japan would result in millions of deaths, United States President Harry Truman authorised the dropping of atomic bombs on Hiroshima and Nagasaki. The devastation and loss of life appalled all Japan.

Ending the Sphere

On 10 August 1945 Emperor Hirohito directed the government to surrender. Six days later the war ended. Japanese officials signed the surrender documents aboard USS *Missouri* in Tokyo Bay on 2 September.

Dazed, the Japanese were now confronted by foreign occupation of their country. General Douglas MacArthur was made Supreme Commander, Allied Powers. Japan accepted the situation peacefully because the emperor instructed them to do so.

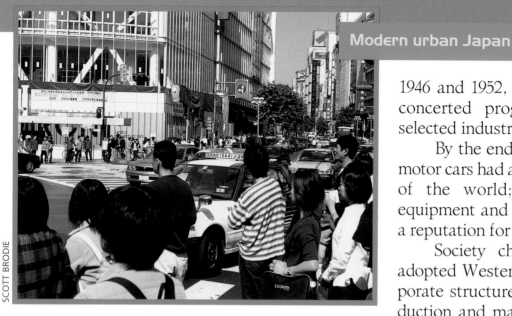

SCOTT BRODIE

1946 and 1952, Japan embarked on a concerted program of developing selected industries.

By the end of the 1950s Japanese motor cars had appeared on the streets of the world; cameras, electrical equipment and watches were gaining a reputation for quality and reliability.

Society changed too. Business adopted Western-style dress and corporate structures. Revolutionary production and management techniques were adopted with great success.

Growth, growth, growth

By the 1970s Japanese quality and value were driving less well made Western goods off the market. Japanese cars, with their reliability and superior fittings, quickly became favourites in many nations. By the 1980s Japanese corporations were building factories across the world.

The economic miracle lasted all the way to the 1990s without faltering. Despite often poor and corrupt government, economic growth was stunning. Japan had one of the highest standards of living in the world and unemployment was almost unknown.

However, the crunch came in the 1990s. With faltering world demand and slowing growth, many corporations were in difficulty. They began cutting costs and retrenching employees. Many Japanese were unable to cope with this new and frightening situation. Corporations collapsed and the nation's inefficient banking system was put under close scrutiny. Lacklustre political leadership has so far failed to return the nation to its previous prosperity.

The occupation

MacArthur began a wholesale restructuring of society. Militarists were purged from the government and civil service, the army was all but disbanded. MacArthur used Hirohito, whose divine status had been officially terminated, to ensure the changes were accepted.

Major land reform was instituted and the Diet was fully democratised. The occupation lasted until April 1952. In 1956 Japan was admitted as a full member of the United Nations.

Dramatic change

Following World War II, Japan's peaceful transformation into a world manufacturing and economic power was astounding. Helped by large amounts of US aid between

www.sources

www.askasia.org/frclasrm/readings/t000013.htm
Timelines of Japanese history

www.lib.duke.edu/ias/eac/histwww.htm
Links to historical sites

web.uccs.edu/~history/index/japan.html
Numerous Japanese history resources

Statistics

Total population
126 780 000
Birth rate
10 per 1000 population
Death rate
8.3 per 1000 population
Infant mortality rate
4 per 1000 live births
Life expectancy
male 78 years
female 84 years

GDP growth rate 1.3%
GDP per capita US$24 900
GDP by sector
agriculture 2%
industry 35%
services 63%

Government revenues
US$441 billion
Government expenditures
US$781 billion

Labour force 68 million
Labour force by sector
agriculture 5%
industry 30%
services 65%
Unemployment rate 5%

Land area 374 744 sq km
Lowest point
Hachiro-gata — -4 m
Highest point
Mount Fuji — 3776 m

Natural resources
minor minerals, fish
Primary industries
sugar beets, vegetables, fruit,
pork, dairy products, eggs, fish,
rice, poultry

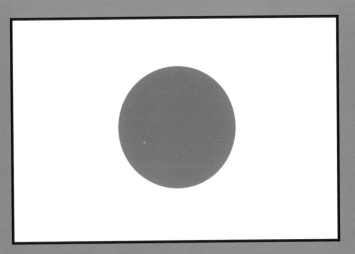

Japan's flag dates from the fourteenth century and is called Hinomaru, which means disc of the sun. The red signifies sincerity and warmth, while the white is for purity. The red disc can also represent Amaterasu Omikami, the Shinto sun goddess.

Secondary industries
motor vehicles, machine tools,
steel, non-ferrous metals, ships,
chemicals, textiles, processed
foods, electronic equipment

Exports US$450 billion
Major exports
motor vehicles, semiconductors,
office equipment, chemicals
Imports US$355 billion
Major imports
fuels, foodstuffs, chemicals,
textiles, office equipment,
minerals

Official language
Japanese
Currency
Japanese yen
Religions
Shintoism, Buddhism,
Christianity

Index

Focus on Asia: Japan   ISBN 0 86415 439 9
Published by   Franklin Watts 96 Leonard Street   London EC2A4XD
Created and produced by Trocadero Publishing   Copyright © 2002 S and L Brodie   Printed in Hong Kong